LAND THAT I LOVE
Regions of the United States

NEW ENGLAND

Niccole Bartley

PowerKiDS press™
New York

Published in 2015 by The Rosen Publishing Group, Inc.
29 East 21st Street, New York, NY 10010

First Edition

Editor: Joanne Randolph
Photo Research: Katie Stryker
Book Design: Colleen Bialecki

Photo Credits: Cover CristinaMuraca/Shutterstock.com; p. 4 RobertPlotz/iStock/Thinkstock; p. 5 LeapingRay/iStock/Thinkstock; pp. 6, 9 MPI/Stringer/Archive Photos/Getty Images; pp. 7, 11 Library of Congress Prints and Photographs Division Washington, DC; p. 8 Lambert/Contributor/Hulton Fine Art Collection/Getty Images; p. 10 Kean Collection/Staff/Archive Photos/Getty Images; p. 12 JupiterImages/Photos.com/Thinkstock; p. 13 (top) dmfoss/iStock/Thinkstock; p. 13 (bottom) Carlos Davila/Photographers Choice RF/Getty Images; p. 14 Adam Jones/Visuals Unlimited/Getty Images; p. 15 Mike Powell/Digital Vision/Thinkstock; p. 16 Jorisvo/iStock/Thinkstock; p. 16 (bottom left) Ritu Manoj Jethani/Shutterstock.com; p. 17 (top) lightphoto/iStock/Thinkstock; p. 17 (bottom) Richard Cavalleri/Shutterstock.com; p. 17 (inset) Joyce VIncent/Shutterstock.com; p. 18 Ron Sanford/iStock/Thinkstock; p. 19 Bronwyn8/iStock/Thinkstock; p. 19 (bottom) erniedecker/iStock/Thinkstock; p. 20 Lijuan Guo/iStock/Thinkstock; p. 21 Wallaceweeks/iStock/Thinkstock; p. 22 Edward Lemery/iStock/Thinkstock.com; p. 23 (top) Vivek Nigam/iStock/Thinkstock; p. 23 (bottom) wellesenterprises/iStock/Thinktock; p. 24 Mike Blea/iStock/Thinkstock; pp. 17 (top), 25 Stephen Saks/Photolibrary/Getty Images; p. 25 (bottom) DougLemke/iStock/Thinkstock; p. 26 Lucidio Studio Inc/Photographers Choice/Getty Images; p. 27 RDaniel12/iStock/Thinkstock; p. 28 Education Images/UIG/GettyImages; pp. 16 (bottom left), 29 James L. Stanfield/National Geographic/Getty Images; p. 30 coleong/iStock/Thinkstock.

Library of Congress Cataloging-in-Publication Data

Bartley, Niccole.
New England / by Niccole Bartley. — First edition.
    pages cm. — (Land that I love: regions of the United States)
Includes index.
ISBN 978-1-4777-6849-5 (library binding) — ISBN 978-1-4777-6850-1 (pbk.) —
ISBN 978-1-4777-6634-7 (6-pack)
1. New England—Juvenile literature. I. Title.
F4.3.B37 2015
974—dc23
                                        2013051014

Manufactured in the United States of America

CPSIA Compliance Information: Batch # WS14PK9: For Further Information contact Rosen Publishing, New York, New York at 1-800-237-9932

CONTENTS

New England is made up of six states. These states are Massachusetts, Maine, New Hampshire, Vermont, Rhode Island, and Connecticut. New England borders the Atlantic Ocean to the east. It is the smallest **region** in the United States, and yet it is also one of the most populated. Most people live near the coast and in the southern New England states.

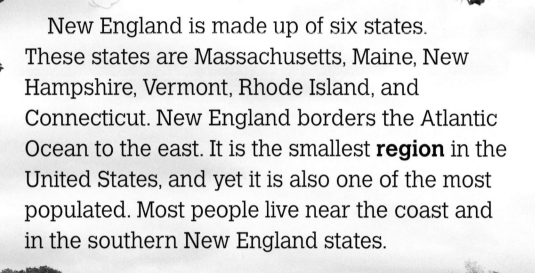

Many people think of rural landscapes and fall foliage, or leaves, when they think of New England.

New England is also known for its beautiful marshlands along the coast. This marsh is on Cape Cod.

Many New Englanders enjoy summers on the coast or at one of the region's many lakes. They spend winters skiing and enjoying other winter sports at ski resorts in the mountains. New Englanders have a strong regional identity. This means people who live in New England have a strong connection to the place where they live.

MORE ABOUT NEW ENGLAND

New England is smaller in total area than the other regions in the United States. The entire region is only slightly larger than Washington State. Rhode Island is the smallest state in New England and in the country. Maine is the largest New England state.

The Algonquians were the earliest-known Native American people to live in New England. The most famous Algonquian tribes in New England were the Wampanoags, Penobscots, Pequots, Mohegans, and Pocumtucks.

Most Algonquians lived in villages of a few hundred people. They moved their camps each season to follow food sources. In warm weather, they lived in **wigwams** near the coast. The men caught fish, whales, and seals in canoes and grew corn, beans, and squash. The women and children gathered shellfish, berries, and nuts.

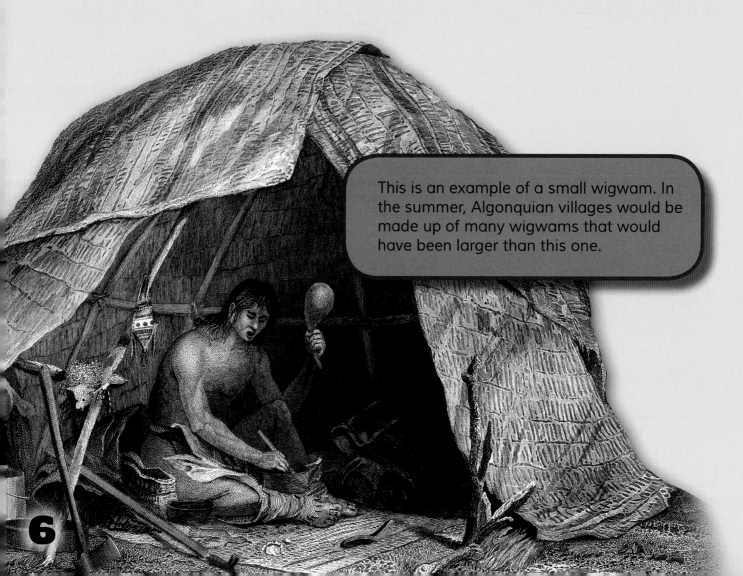

This is an example of a small wigwam. In the summer, Algonquian villages would be made up of many wigwams that would have been larger than this one.

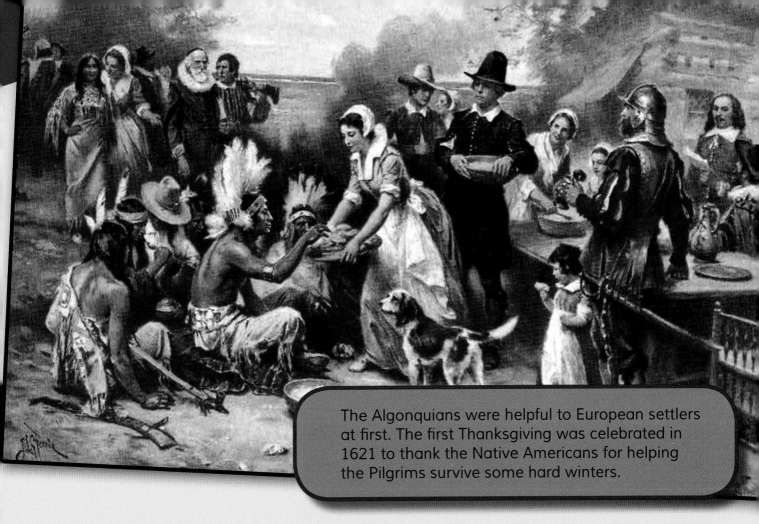

The Algonquians were helpful to European settlers at first. The first Thanksgiving was celebrated in 1621 to thank the Native Americans for helping the Pilgrims survive some hard winters.

In cool weather, they moved into wooden longhouses in the forests and ate food they had stored or hunted animals like white-tailed deer and moose.

There were around 100,000 Native Americans living in New England in the 1600s when the Europeans arrived. In less than a hundred years, there were fewer than 10,000 left.

A WAMPANOAG LEGEND: MOSHUP THE GIANT

There is a legend among the Wampanoag tribe about a giant named Moshup. Moshup lived among the Wampanoag Indians on Martha's Vineyard. He loved whale meat and caught whales with his bare hands. Moshup shared his whale meat with the Wampanoags. In return, they gave him all of the tobacco they grew. He smoked it in his great pipe and dumped the ashes into the sea, creating the island of Nantucket.

NEW ENGLAND HISTORY

The earliest European settlers of New England were English. In 1620, a ship called the *Mayflower* carried a group of settlers called Pilgrims from England to the shores of present-day Cape Cod, Massachusetts. The Pilgrims came to the **New World** in search of religious freedom. This was just the first of many such groups that came to New England.

Here the Pilgrims are landing at Plymouth, Massachusetts. The Pilgrims named their settlement Plymouth Colony. Over half of the passengers of the *Mayflower* died the first winter in Plymouth.

The Boston Massacre was one of the events that led up to the American Revolution. British soldiers shot into a crowd of protesting colonists, killing five people.

The Puritans arrived in present-day Boston 10 years later and established the Massachusetts Bay Colony. These settlers were well-known for their hard work and strict, religious lifestyle.

The settlers and the Native Americans got along at first, but soon fights broke out over the land. In the end, much of the native population was killed or pushed out of New England.

By the late 1700s, many more colonies had been settled along the East Coast. Eventually, these colonies came to want their independence from Britain. They got their wish after fighting the **American Revolution** to become the United States of America.

Hundreds of factories were built during the Industrial Revolution. This is the Oriental Powder Mill, in Maine, which made gunpowder.

For much of the 1700s and 1800s, whaling was a major New England industry. It reached its peak in 1846, with some 736 ships whaling in America. The last whaler was sent out of New Bedford, Massachusetts, in 1927.

In the 1800s, New England became a leader in the **Industrial Revolution**. Many factories were built. **Immigrants** from Europe continued to arrive in New England, especially from Ireland, Italy, and Portugal. New England continues to have a **diverse** population today.

WRITE ABOUT IT!

Pretend you are a child whose father was off fighting in the American Revolution. Do some research on what daily life would have been like and then send a letter to your father about what you are doing while he is away.

COASTAL COMMUNITY

New England has many quaint coastal towns along the Atlantic seaboard that were founded by the English settlers. In the time of the settlers, the coast was rich with shellfish and **migratory** birds. The cold waters of the Atlantic were filled with fish, especially cod. Soon towns were built around the harbors. New England's whaling and trading industries were born. Some of New England's best-known exports are still lobsters and cod.

Many people have come to this beach in Rhode Island to swim and surf.

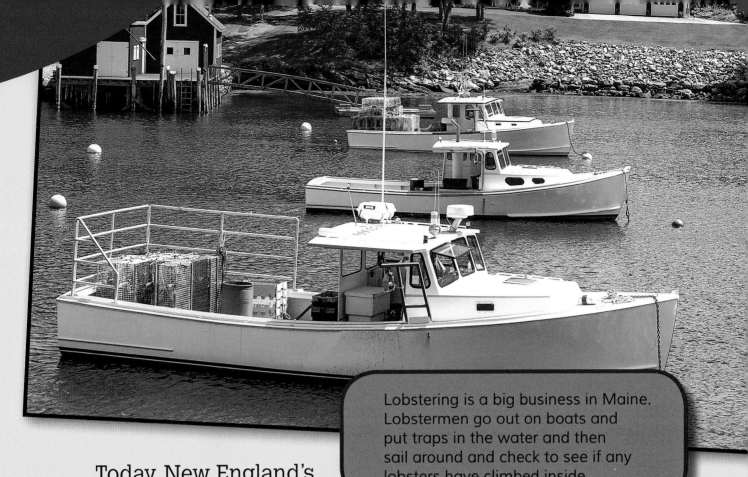

Lobstering is a big business in Maine. Lobstermen go out on boats and put traps in the water and then sail around and check to see if any lobsters have climbed inside.

Today, New England's coastal areas are popular tourist destinations in the summer. Cape Cod, Martha's Vineyard, and Nantucket have some of the loveliest beaches in the United States. Some important New England coastal port cities and towns are Boston, Massachusetts, Newport, Rhode Island, and Bar Harbor and Portland, Maine.

Though there are far fewer whales now than when settlers first arrived on the East Coast, people still enjoy taking whale-watching trips off the coast of New England to see humpback, finback, right, and minke whales.

The mountain ranges of New England were formed 18,000 years ago by glaciers. The glaciers moved through the region and left behind mountains, rolling hills, and many ponds and lakes. The mountains are covered in forests of pine, maple, birch, and oak trees. Many types of wildlife can be found in New England, especially moose, deer, and bears.

The White Mountains are home to Mount Washington, the highest peak in the Northeast. Mount Washington is named after the first president of the United States and is said to have the world's worst weather most of the year.

Families enjoy hiking on the many mountain trails throughout New England.

The White Mountains, the Berkshire Mountains, and the Green Mountains are part of the Appalachian mountain range. The Appalachian range runs along the East Coast of the United States from Georgia to Maine. New Englanders have learned to enjoy the mountains by skiing in the winter and hiking and biking in summer.

NEW ENGLAND'S WATERWAYS

The Connecticut River valley and the Merrimack Valley are the most important valleys of New England. The longest river is the Connecticut River. It flows from New Hampshire to New York. New England is home to many lakes and ponds. Lake Champlain in Vermont, Moosehead Lake in Maine, and Lake Winnipesaukee in New Hampshire are the largest lakes in New England. Historically, people like to settle near rivers, lakes, and ponds since they give access to fresh water and can be helpful in transporting goods.

NEW ENGLAND

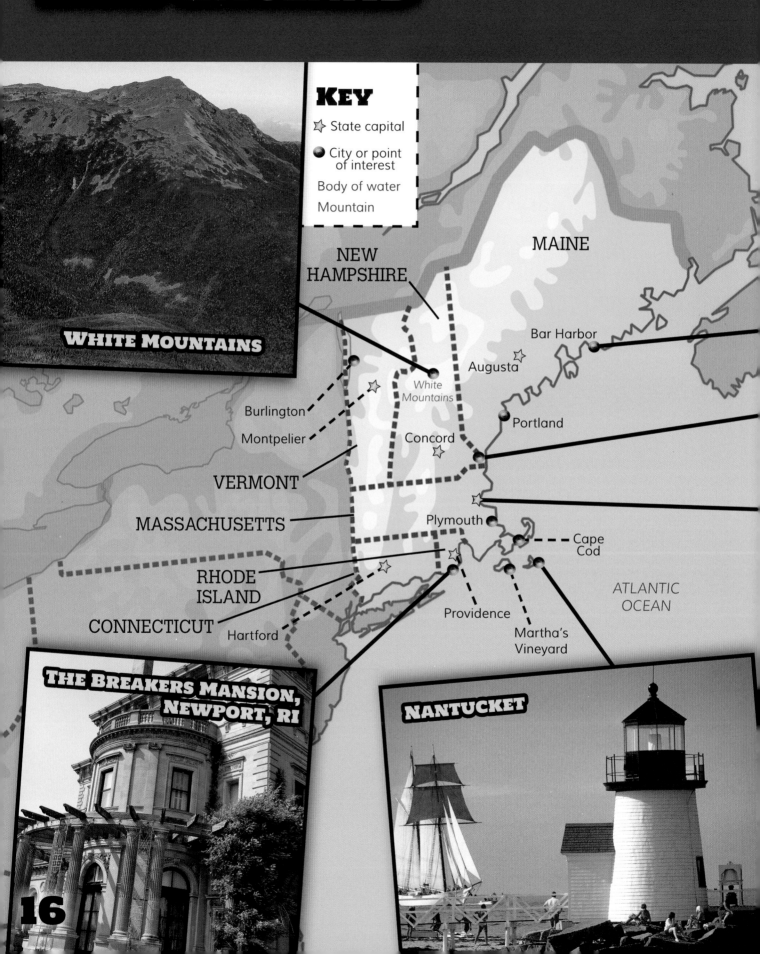

KEY
⭐ State capital
🔴 City or point of interest
Body of water
Mountain

WHITE MOUNTAINS

MAINE

NEW HAMPSHIRE

Bar Harbor

Augusta

White Mountains

Portland

Burlington

Montpelier

Concord

VERMONT

MASSACHUSETTS

Plymouth

Cape Cod

RHODE ISLAND

CONNECTICUT

Hartford

Providence

Martha's Vineyard

ATLANTIC OCEAN

THE BREAKERS MANSION, NEWPORT, RI

NANTUCKET

ACADIA NATIONAL PARK

STRAWBERY BANKE, PORTSMOUTH, NH

BOSTON, MA

FENWAY PARK

17

PLANTS AND ANIMALS OF THE REGION

When the first European explorers arrived in New England, the land was mostly forests that were filled with many different plants and animals. By the mid-1800s, only 30 to 40 percent of New England was forestland. The rest was cleared for farming or lumber. There has been a big recovery in New England's forests. Today, almost 80 percent of the region is again covered in forests. New England is also known for its wild blueberries, cranberries, and blackberries that often grow on riverbanks and the edges of forests.

Moose are probably one of the most unusual animals in the region. Moose can weigh 900 to 1,000 pounds (408–454 kg)!

New England is known for its fall apple picking. There are orchards throughout the region that allow people to pick their own apples.

With the return of the forests, native animals, such as deer, wild turkeys, beavers, and moose are thriving. Bears are back, too, and so are gray seals, eagles, woodpeckers, and hawks.

Milk snakes are at home in the forests and rocky hillsides of New England.

NATURAL RESOURCES AND INDUSTRY

In the early days, New England settlers were mostly farmers and homesteaders. New Englanders found it difficult to farm because of the unfertile, rocky soil and cold climate. The early Colonial settlers were known for their **self-reliance**. Soon, the large number of natural resources such as forests, streams, and harbors brought new industries such as shipbuilding, fishing, and trade across the Atlantic Ocean. Whaling was a major industry in the 1700s and 1800s. Whale oil was used for lighting, cosmetics, and countless other products.

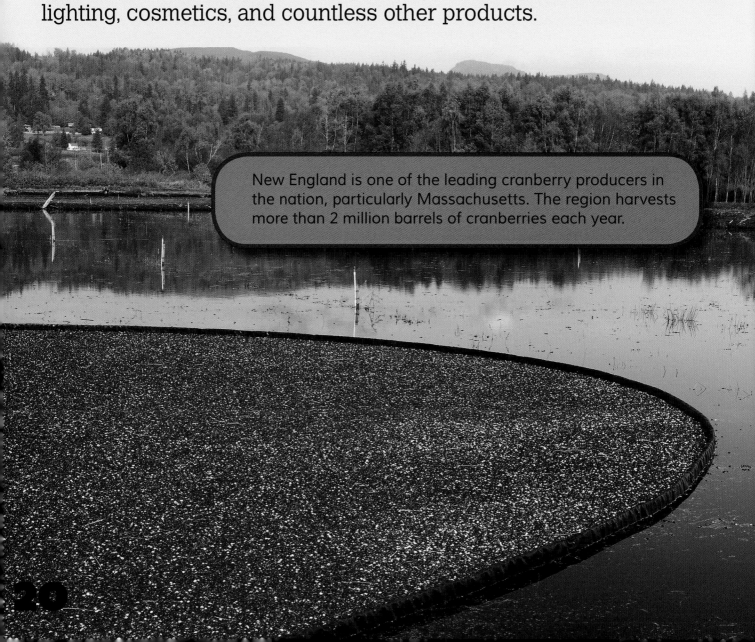

New England is one of the leading cranberry producers in the nation, particularly Massachusetts. The region harvests more than 2 million barrels of cranberries each year.

Fishing and lobstering are major New England industries.

By the 1800s, the Industrial Revolution arrived in America. Factories were built all over Massachusetts, Connecticut, and Rhode Island. The most important natural resource products of New England still remain granite, lobster, and cod.

A LEADER IN EDUCATION

New England has long been known as a leader in education. Many of the best universities and colleges in the nation were founded here, including Harvard, Yale, Brown, Dartmouth, Wellesley, Amherst, and many others. Today, New England remains a leader in education, medicine, finance, and technology.

NEW ENGLAND CITIES

The major cities in New England are Boston, Massachusetts, Providence, Rhode Island, Hartford and New Haven, Connecticut, Burlington, Vermont, Manchester and Portsmouth, New Hampshire, and Portland, Maine. Boston is the capital of Massachusetts and the largest city in New England. Boston is also one of the oldest cities in the United States. Boston has many colleges and universities. The city is famous for the Freedom Trail, which is a walking tour through many historic places from the American Revolution.

Boston and the surrounding area, which includes Quincy and Cambridge, is the largest metropolitan area in New England.

Hartford is home to the nation's oldest public art museum, the oldest public park, and the oldest newspaper. Mark Twain, the famous author, is also from Hartford and his family home is now a museum.

Providence is the capital of Rhode Island and was one of the first cities established in the United States. There are many cobblestone streets in Providence.

Hartford is the capital of Connecticut. Hartford is known for being home to many insurance companies.

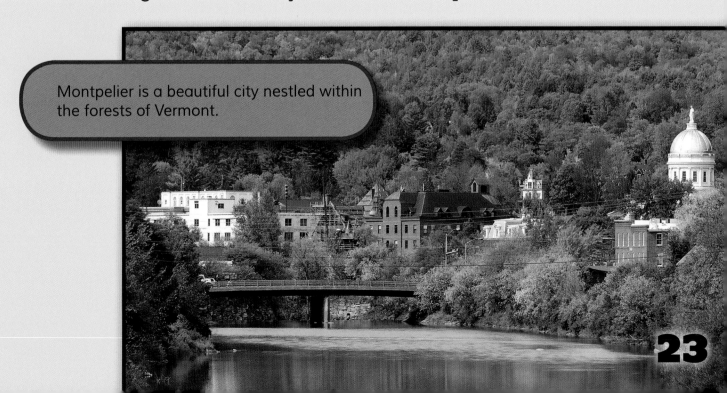

Montpelier is a beautiful city nestled within the forests of Vermont.

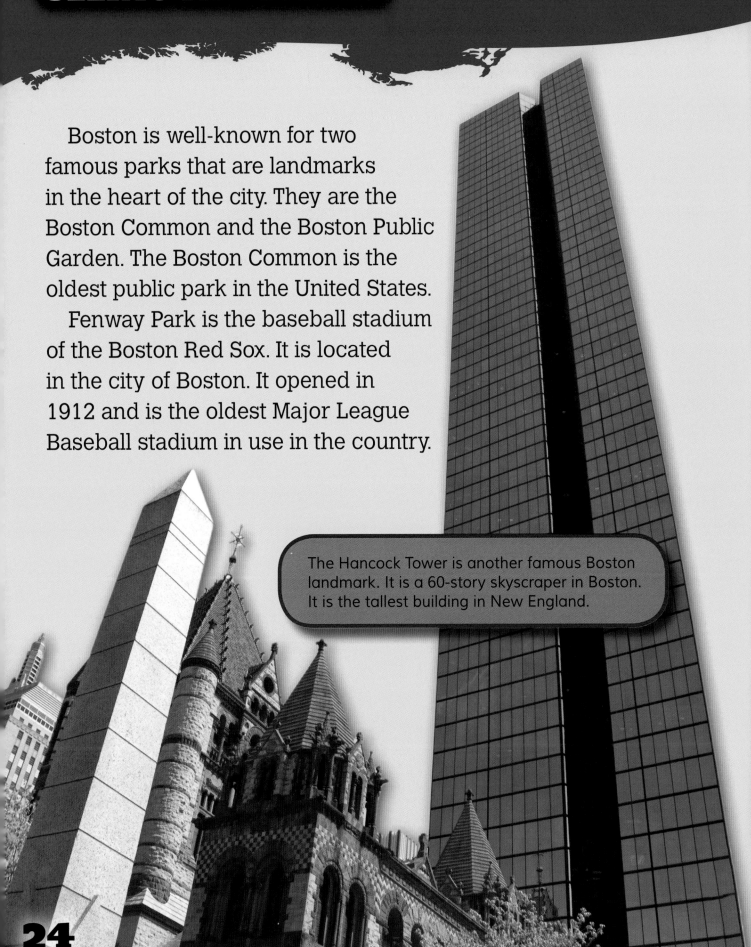

Boston is well-known for two famous parks that are landmarks in the heart of the city. They are the Boston Common and the Boston Public Garden. The Boston Common is the oldest public park in the United States.

Fenway Park is the baseball stadium of the Boston Red Sox. It is located in the city of Boston. It opened in 1912 and is the oldest Major League Baseball stadium in use in the country.

The Hancock Tower is another famous Boston landmark. It is a 60-story skyscraper in Boston. It is the tallest building in New England.

Strawbery Banke is the oldest neighborhood in Portsmouth, New Hampshire. It was settled by the English in 1630. It is named after the wild berries that grew along the river. Today it is an outdoor museum.

The Newport Mansions, in the seaside town of Newport, Rhode Island, are a famous New England landmark. Built in the 1850s, the nation's wealthiest families summered in Newport and built grand mansions with elaborate ballrooms.

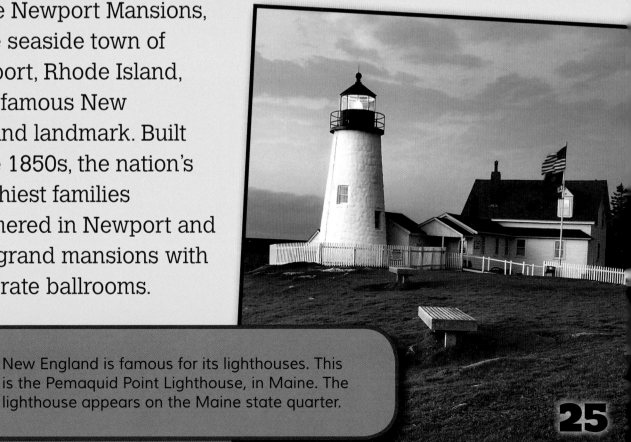

New England is famous for its lighthouses. This is the Pemaquid Point Lighthouse, in Maine. The lighthouse appears on the Maine state quarter.

Many New Englanders enjoy hiking, biking, and kayaking. New Englanders also love sports. The most famous sports teams in the region are the Boston Red Sox, the New England Patriots, the Boston Celtics, and the Boston Bruins.

Fall is a special time in New England when people remember their heritage and historic moments such as the first Thanksgiving. Pumpkin picking is a traditional fall event.

Ice-skating is a popular New England pastime that makes the most of the cold winter weather.

New Englanders enjoy food and have a special regional cuisine. They love apple cider during the fall, clambakes in the summer, and pancakes with maple syrup all the time. New England is a great place to find blueberries, cranberries, and lobster. New England clam chowder is a favorite regional dish.

Vermont is home to many dairy farms. They produce fine cheeses and other dairy products. Waterbury, Vermont, is the official home of Ben & Jerry's ice cream. The small coastal town of Rockland is known as the lobster capital of Maine. Each August, the town hosts the Maine Lobster Festival.

New England has more than 200 historic lighthouses. Many people enjoy visiting and collecting photographs of these historic lighthouses.

New England is also famous for its covered bridges. Covered bridges are a beautiful part of the New England landscape and people love to bike or drive through the region to see the bridges. Fall is a popular time to make this trip so New Englanders can also enjoy the beautiful fall foliage.

The Boston Marathon is an important yearly event in New England. Thousands of runners from all over the world come to run and enjoy the sights of New England.

New England's many lighthouses are an icon of the area. They were once lit by whale oil, but most are now automated. Here the historic ship *Shenandoah* sails past Brant Point Light, on Nantucket.

REGIONAL RECIPES:
TASTE OF NEW ENGLAND

New England produces lots of maple syrup in the late winter and early spring. Make these homemade pancakes and top them with warm maple syrup from New England!

Pancakes with maple syrup

Ingredients
1 1/2 cups all-purpose flour
3 1/2 teaspoons baking powder
1 teaspoon salt
1 tablespoon white sugar
1 1/4 cups milk
1 egg
3 tablespoons butter, melted
1 cup New England maple syrup, warmed

DIRECTIONS:
1. In a large bowl, mix together the flour, baking powder, salt, and sugar. Make a well in the center and pour in the milk, egg, and melted butter. Mix until smooth.
2. Heat a lightly oiled griddle or frying pan over medium high heat. Pour or scoop the batter onto the griddle, using approximately 1/4 cup for each pancake. Brown on both sides and serve hot with warm maple syrup.

New England is a region that is rich in history and natural beauty. Europeans who arrived in America from the 1600s to 1800s made the region what it is today.

New England is small in size but has a large, diverse population and rich culture that is distinct from the rest of the United States. Much of the original spirit of New England remains in the region, from the small New England port towns on the Atlantic Coast to the rolling hills and mountains to the west and north.

Boston's Beacon Hill is famous for its beautiful old brownstones.

GLOSSARY

American Revolution (uh-MER-uh-ken reh-vuh-LOO-shun) Battles that soldiers from the colonies fought against Britain for freedom, from 1775 to 1783.

diverse (dy-VERS) Different.

Industrial Revolution (in-DUS-tree-ul reh-vuh-LOO-shun) A time in history beginning in the mid-1700s, when power-driven machines were first used to produce goods in large quantities, changing the way people lived and worked.

immigrants (IH-muh-grunts) People who move to a new country from another country.

migratory (MY-gruh-tor-ee) Moving from one place to another.

New World (NOO WURLD) North America and South America.

region (REE-jun) One of the different parts of Earth.

self-reliance (SELF-rih-LY-unts) The ability to do things for oneself.

wigwams (WIG-wahmz) Domed Native American shelters.

INDEX

WEBSITES

Due to the changing nature of Internet links, PowerKids Press has developed an online list of websites related to the subject of this book. This site is updated regularly. Please use this link to access the list:

www.powerkidslinks.com/ltil/engl/